Praise for Teachers Are Heroes™

"Mark Anthony Garrett validates the decision I made to become an educator. I've seen him three times and I recommend him highly."

— Jim Frazier, Superintendent
Brown County

"Mark Anthony Garrett has given us a powerful gift in his book Teachers Are Heroes. Not only is it a celebration of the profession and the difference teachers make, it is a guide for showing teachers how to truly transform the lives of those they teach."

— Chike Akua, Executive Director
Teacher Transformation Institute

"Mark Anthony Garrett has truly captured the essence of what real teaching is all about."

— Dr. Robert L. Lawson, Educator

"When I heard Mark Anthony Garrett present his Teachers Are Heroes message, I was totally blown away. I have been a conference planner for many years and Mark is one of the BEST SPEAKERS I've ever seen and one of the best at connecting with an audience. I was so impressed that I invited him to be the opening keynote speaker at our State Title One conference. I would highly recommend him to any school district who is looking for someone to inspire and recharge their educators."

— Bill Bogner, Title One Conference Facilitator
OAASFEP

Teachers Are Heroes:

7 Success Principles For Transformational Teaching

By Mark Anthony Garrett
©2013

To my Third Grade Teacher,
Mrs. Ritchie,
who is and will always be my hero.

Acknowledgements

At this moment, I would like to thank some of the individuals that have been critical in my life's journey and success. Without these wonderful people, I would not be the man that I am today.

I am forever grateful and I extend my deepest gratitude and thanks to My Lord and Savior for without him nothing is possible.

My wonderful and beautiful wife Tracee. Thank you for seeing my potential and always believing in me, even when I did not believe in myself.

To my children, Halston, Mark, Braden and Myles, who are sometimes my greatest teachers.

To my brother Victor and his loving wife Patricia for guiding me in the right direction while growing up.

To my late parents, Marion and Mary Garrett.

To my best friend and mentor Dr. Robert L. Lawson, thanks for the many late nights of brainstorming and building the dream.

To Chike Akua, thank you for believing in this project and encouraging me to get it done.

To Kendall Lee and Melissa Thompson, for the opportunity to truly spread my wings and fly.

To Harvey Alston, the mentor's mentor. Thank you for teaching me how to dance with who brought me.

To my staff, thanks for all of your hard work, you guys ROCK!

To Aleta Polley, thanks for your friendship and introducing me to the world of public speaking.

Last but not least, to my dear friends and mentors Gail Spears and Bobby Cochran. Your love and support have blessed my life in so many ways. I love you both unconditionally.

Mark Anthony Garrett

For more information about

Teachers Are Heroes

please visit us at:

www.TeachersAreHeroes.com

Table of Contents

Preface

It was a cold winter morning in Detroit at a large educational conference. I was burdened down with large boxes of books and DVDs at a huge convention center. I didn't know my way around, where to park, where to unload, which room to present in, or even what to do. I was completely disoriented as the time for my presentation drew nearer and nearer. I slowly exhaled and watched my breath break against the cold air. As I was feeling my heart rate rise, a man suddenly appeared.

"Hey man, do you need a hand," he asked. Relieved, I smiled. "Yeah, definitely! Thanks." I replied. The man picked up several boxes and we headed toward the convention center. While walking through the expansive space, we discovered that he was to present in the room right next to mine. "Thanks again ..." I paused, awaiting him to tell me his name. "Mark Anthony Garrett." He replied. "Well, thanks again, Mark Anthony Garrett." We shook hands one more time and he headed over to his room. I then realized I was truly in the presence of a great man—this was indeed someone who had a natural gift for helping people.

I had no idea that Mark was a nationally known speaker and trainer, and he was so selflessly willing to assist me. Imagine that! He could have been relaxing or preparing for his own presentation. But to see someone in need and not help is not his way.

After my presentation, I decided to sit in on his session. To say I was amazed would be an understatement. He didn't give a speech, he created an experience. As his presentation ended, I noticed the teachers were more excited, informed, inspired and encouraged with new insights and approaches. They left with a newfound ability to connect with their children as well as to increase their student achievement.

Since becoming good friends, I have seen him teach this experience in many cities, settings and demographics. Mark has a way of connecting with people that transcends culture, class, background, and socioeconomic status. And whether speaking to teachers, foster care workers or the children themselves, the result is always a fun, high-energy transformational experience.

Needless to say, I was very flattered and humbled when Mark asked me to write the introduction to his book *Teachers Are Heroes*. During our many conversations on the content of this book, I realized this book is much needed and long overdue.

In my book, ***Education for Transformation***, I discuss the fact that the oldest word relative to teaching and learning comes out of the Nile Valley of Africa. The word is Seba and it has three primary meanings, "teach," "door," and "star." Along with other evidence, this indicates that the most ancient philosophy of education is, "The teacher opens the door to the universe so the student may shine like a star." And this is precisely what Mark Anthony Garrett does!

Whether speaking to "at-risk youth" or educators, Mark always opens the door to new worlds of possibilities, he lifts the spirit of his audiences and shows them how to shine. And he's been doing this consistently, nationally and internationally for over 20 years now.

The ancient sage Ptahhotep goes on to further describe what Seba do: "The Seba feeds the soul with that which endures unto eternity." Again, this is a fitting description of the powerful work Mark Anthony Garrett does. He has literally saved the lives of countless youth (by their own admission), whose lives have been ravaged by physical, emotional and sexual abuse, neglect, family separation, incarceration, poverty and terminal illness. He feeds the souls of those he serves because he is intuitively in-tune with their suffering. For, to look at him now, no one would imagine that he has experienced in some form or fashion several of the afore-mentioned litany of devastating life situations. These are just a few of the things that make him uniquely qualified to write this book.

So it seems only fitting that now he would carefully and lovingly share the secrets that make teachers heroes in the lives of the students and communities they serve. I am blessed and honored to know Mark Anthony Garrett and I invite you to go on an engaging journey in the following pages to meet the hero within you!

Chike Akua, Executive Director
Teacher Transformation Institute
Conyers, GA
June, 2013

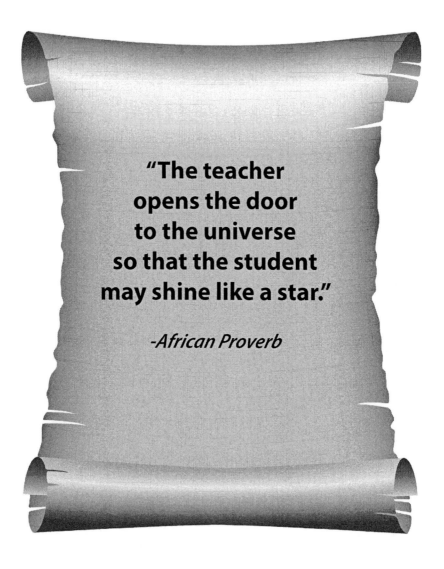

"The teacher
opens the door
to the universe
so that the student
may shine like a star."

-African Proverb

Foreword

My name is Dr. Robert L. Lawson and I am a teacher and lifelong educator. As someone who has spent the past 40 years involved in the field of education, it is indeed a tremendous honor and privilege to be asked to write the foreword for this amazing book. Mark Anthony Garrett has truly captured the essence of what real teaching is all about.

Our hats are off to all of the teachers around the world. You truly do an amazing and incredible job going into those classrooms day after day. It is not an easy task and you are to be commended for your hard work. There is no question about the fact that you truly are the heroes of today. Where would we be without you?

As you read this book, I warn you, get prepared to be motivated, inspired and ready to roll, because as you turn each page, you are going to discover one captivating story after another or one amazing quote after another or something else that causes you to realize that you truly do make a difference in the lives of others.

Had it not been for you, there are people in our society who would not even be alive today were it not for your encouragement and your involvement in the lives of your students. As Mark Anthony Garrett says in the text of his book, sometimes, teaching is a thankless job. There may be times when you are teaching your heart out and it may seem that no one cares. Reading this book helps you to realize that it is at those moments that you could really be making a positive difference in someone's life. Maybe no one will ever come back and tell you what you did that made a difference.

What's important here is that you keep on keeping on and do what you do best in the classroom. Students may not always know how to convey how they feel about the difference you are making in their lives. They may never come back and say *thank you* but just know deep down in your heart that the primary reason why you got into this business in the first place was so you could help someone. Your knowledge of that is all that matters.

Dr. Robert L. Lawson
Lifetime Educator,
Teacher

Teachers are Heroes
By Dr. Robert L. Lawson

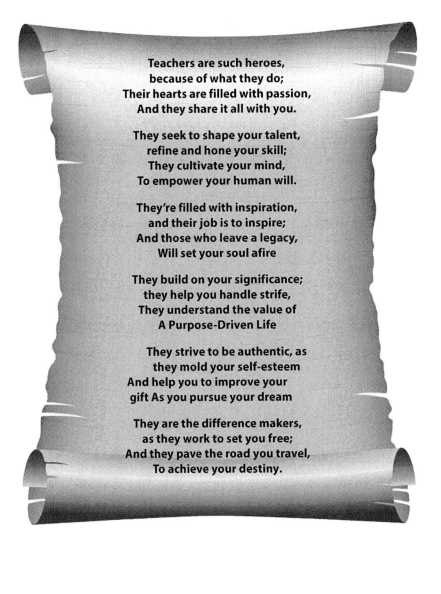

Teachers are such heroes,
because of what they do;
Their hearts are filled with passion,
And they share it all with you.

They seek to shape your talent,
refine and hone your skill;
They cultivate your mind,
To empower your human will.

They're filled with inspiration,
and their job is to inspire;
And those who leave a legacy,
Will set your soul afire

They build on your significance;
they help you handle strife,
They understand the value of
A Purpose-Driven Life

They strive to be authentic, as
they mold your self-esteem
And help you to improve your
gift As you pursue your dream

They are the difference makers,
as they work to set you free;
And they pave the road you travel,
To achieve your destiny.

Introduction

It's a miracle that I'm even alive. As a kid who was abandoned by a drug-addicted mother, placed in foster care, placed in special education, suffered repeated physical and sexual abuse, was a drug dealer and drug user, it is amazing to me that I've lived to tell the story. Who would imagine after all of the trials and tribulations, the ups, downs, ins, outs, twists and turns my life has taken—who would imagine that I would now be the one to inspire thousands of teachers, students labeled "at-risk" and their caregivers around the country and even internationally? To look at me now, you would never imagine that my past was so horrific. And yet none of this would be possible if it hadn't been for one teacher in third grade who transformed my life. I am the product of an incredible teacher's miraculous teaching.

So it is my privilege, with deep respect and a sense of profound pride and reverence that I write this book in honor of my third grade teacher, Mrs. Betty Jean Ritchie, and to every teacher in the world who takes pride in his/her work and cares about young people. You see, I found out a long time ago that it really does all boil down to caring. The old adage is quite true. "Kids don't care how much you know until they know how much you care."

It is my opinion that teachers are not given the adequate respect they deserve for the amazing and incredible jobs they do on a daily basis. They are over-worked and underpaid and yet, they are the ones who, day after day, go into those classrooms and do what they do best. You see, it is as David Haselkorn has said. "Teaching is the profession that makes all other professions possible."

How is it that at the lowest point in my life—the point that I was about to take my own life as a troubled teen—that Mrs. Ritchie's words (spoken a decade earlier from that day) would ring in my ears and keep me from doing the unthinkable. This is why I say teachers are heroes and why I have chosen to write this book. I work with some of the most challenging students in our society—foster children, students with learning disabilities, victims of abuse, behavior disorders, depression and every disadvantage imaginable. The one thing they are all looking for is someone who believes in them and cares enough to help them navigate through life's challenges.

As I travel around the country speaking and training teachers and as I examine the educational landscape of America, it is my opinion that teachers are not placed in a high enough regard as they should be. They spend more time with the children than their own parents. Indeed, teachers are heroes.

In addition, the challenges teachers face today are enormous—salary and budget cuts, class and school overcrowding, parents who have gone AWOL, high-stakes testing, sweeping cultural and economic shifts in society. Yet teachers show up day after day to mold and shape the minds of tomorrow.

If you are a teacher who is committed, loves children and teaching, then this book is for you. You will find examples of how you can further master the craft of teaching. However, if you are a teacher who is feeling the pressures of burnout and wondering if you're making a difference; if you're even thinking about changing professions because you feel you're not cut out for this kind of work or not able to truly reach and teach the children—hang on. This book is for you, too. You're a hero, too, you just don't know it yet.

Every few pages you will see a statement in a rectangle with bold print that says, "Teachers are Heroes because…" Pay particular attention to these statements. You will also see scrolls with powerful, life-changing quotes on them. Give special attention to these also.

If you'll bear with me, I'd like to share the success principles that make great teachers great. I'd also like to share how Ms. Ritchie embodied and employed these principles to transform my life far beyond the years that I was in her class. You see, I'm the kid everyone gave up on. Picture your most difficult student— you know, the one who can't sit still in class, the one who causes disruption, the one who runs his mouth a little too much and talks back; the one who is withdrawn from time to time, seemingly for no reason. *When you see that kid in your class, that's me. So I need you to know there's more to that child than meets the eye.* I also need you to know that you are deeply significant in the life of that child and all of your students.

It is my hope that this book brings you motivation, inspiration and critical information to help make you an even greater hero in the lives of your students.

Principle 1

Purpose:
Understand Your Reason For Being:
Your Purpose is Powerful

Teachers are Heroes because they serve with a spirit of excellence.

I'll never forget my first day of school at Kittyhawk Elementary School. My foster father had driven me to school in the big station wagon and we were running a little late. After he parked, my dad took my hand and we walked through the big, brown metal doors. We didn't know which way to go. We were soon directed to the office.

I was apprehensive and a little anxious starting a new school and a new school year. Who would be in my class? Would I make some new friends? Who would my teacher be? As I saw other students in the hallway on their way to class, it became clear very quickly that I was one of the few black kids in the school.

As we walked through the halls, trying to find our way, we were greeted by a warm and wonderful woman. She was slim and her brown hair was not quite to her shoulders. She wore slacks with a bright, colorful blouse.

"Hello," she said to my father in a cheerful voice. Then she looked down at me. "And who is this handsome young man?" she asked holding out her hand. My hand fit naturally into her hand. I smiled shyly.

My father introduced himself and me. I felt proud that she had called me handsome. That first meeting with Mrs. Ritchie produced a spark within me. She captured my attention and made me feel good about myself.

Why did you decide to become a teacher? This is a question whose answer reveals your purpose and it is a question that you must visit and revisit from time to time. The answer to this question will be the driving force behind your success as a teacher. Maybe there was a special teacher in your life and you want to have that

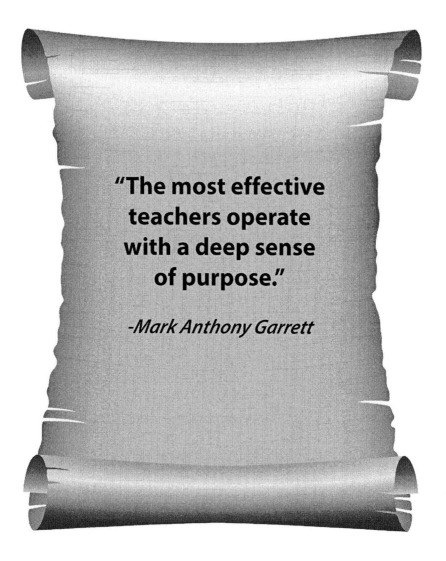

"The most effective teachers operate with a deep sense of purpose."

-Mark Anthony Garrett

effect on children. Maybe you *didn't* have a special teacher and want to be the type of teacher you never had. Maybe you were the type of child who always loved school and you wanted to teach other children just like you. Maybe you were a student who struggled and you want to be able to reach students who share the same struggles you did.

The most effective teachers operate with a deep sense of purpose. They are quick to share that their reason for being (RFB) is to help young people be their best—and it shows. It shows in the way these teachers prepare, brainstorm, lesson plan, create, deliver and execute dynamic lessons that capture and inspire the hearts and minds of their students.

But there will be times when you will face some serious challenges as a teacher—students who have trouble grasping concepts, behavior problems, irate, absent or unsupportive parents, etc. When others become discouraged, negative, cynical and sarcastic, you must fall back on your reason for being there—to reach and teach the children. Understanding your purpose will give you the spirit and energy to go the distance.

It seems like some people are simply put on this earth to teach. They have a pleasing personality. They have superior communication skills that captivate and engage everyone under the

Teachers are Heroes because they care.

sound of their voice. They have a genuine joy for what they do and gain increasing fulfillment from working with those they teach. The telltale sign is that children, and people in general, love to be around this type of person. Mrs. Ritchie was one of these kinds of teachers. Make it your mission to be around teachers like this at your school and embody the qualities listed above.

"When the purpose
and vision are clear,
instructional insights
will appear."

- Chike Akua
Educator & Author

Teachers are Heroes because they stimulate untapped potential in others.

Many schools are notorious for "the lounge mafia." Beware. These are instructors who sit in the teachers' lounge doing verbal drive by's on students they do not know how to reach, speaking negatively and sarcastically. Since they cannot reach these students, they label them universally "unreachable" and try to get other instructors to co-sign to their own lack of competence and professionalism. Part of your purpose is to spend as little time in the company of such instructors as possible and to seek and find those educators who care, who understand their purpose and who have a track record of success. If you are not clear about your purpose, you will be consumed and enveloped by the day-to-day challenges and pressures.

Teachers are Heroes because they stimulate untapped potential in others.

One of the tragedies in the systems of education today is that most educators have not had the opportunity to sit under the tutelage and influence of a master teacher or master administrator. Most have not seen a master teacher work with the most challenging students, yet produce stellar and sterling results.

There will be some instructors who try to convince you that some students are just going to fail. Some teachers are resigned to this notion as soon as they see a student for the first time. The self-fulfilling prophecy is very real. But you must realize that there are educators who have a track record of reaching all of their students consistently. For example, Urban Prep High School in Chicago has a 100 percent Black male student population. Their students come from some of the most challenging communities in Chicago.

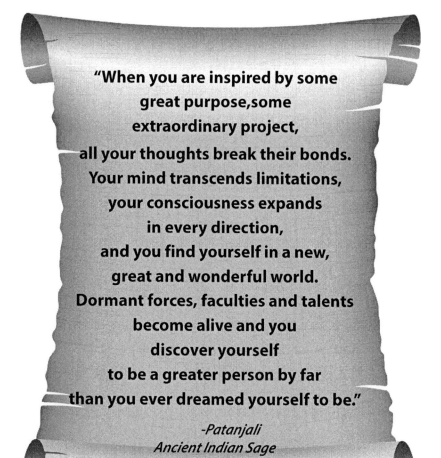

"When you are inspired by some
great purpose,some
extraordinary project,
all your thoughts break their bonds.
Your mind transcends limitations,
your consciousness expands
in every direction,
and you find yourself in a new,
great and wonderful world.
Dormant forces, faculties and talents
become alive and you
discover yourself
to be a greater person by far
than you ever dreamed yourself to be."

-Patanjali
Ancient Indian Sage

However, Urban Prep boasts a 100 percent graduation and college acceptance rate for the past four years straight. How is this possible when the national Black male graduation rate is a mere 52 percent? When Urban Prep started, the national average was a mere 47 percent! It goes back to purpose and vision. The culturally diverse leaders and teachers of the school have made it their purpose to reach and teach every student and ensure that he graduates and gets accepted to college.

Unfortunately, much of what teachers learn about effective teaching in college is obsolete by the time they graduate and enter the classroom. But award-winning educator and author, Chike Akua tells us that, "**when the purpose and vision are clear, instructional insights will appear.**" So if you're in undergraduate school or graduate school, studying to be a teacher, learn all you can from that program,—just be willing to go significantly beyond it if you want to get the results you desire.

The ancient Indian sage, Patanjali, had some powerful and profound things to say about purpose:

> *"When you are inspired by some great **purpose**, some extraordinary project, all your thoughts break their bonds. Your mind transcends limitations, your consciousness expands in every direction, and you find yourself in a new, great and wonderful world. Dormant forces, faculties and talents become alive and you discover yourself to be a greater person by far than you ever dreamed yourself to be."*

The incredible things that will happen that Patanjali so vividly describes, hinges on one thing—purpose. Purpose drives direction. Once the purpose is clear, that is when the "dormant faculties and talents come alive." So, clarity of purpose increases the potency of your power as a teacher. Clarity of purpose is also contagious— it'll rub off on your students. Whereas, at one time you may have had to get them back on track, they will increasingly engage in correcting one another because the purpose is clear.

Although purpose originates from within, it has decided effects on the world and the people who are an integral part of your sphere of influence, particularly your students. When you teach with purpose, you demonstrate a commitment that transcends a paycheck and the power of that commitment is the thing that literally shines through everything you do.

When you teach with a sense of purpose, you are not teaching to a standard and you are not even remotely concerned about whether or not a particular assessment is formative or summative. Your intent is to reach the student because you care about the student. You make a conscientious effort to determine how your students learn best and then you do an adequate job of trying to craft the material in such a way that the students who are in your class can learn something from the experience.

When you teach with a sense of purpose, you send a message to students that you are there, teaching them for a reason. You aren't there because it's a job that pays the bills; you are there primarily because teaching fulfills some inexplicable, essential part of you. It is a calling; it is a devotion much more potent and lasting than simple desire. While this message will likely go unacknowledged, it is not readily apparent to others. It is something though that seeks to operate in a student's subconscious mind as that student understands later in life how committed you were to teaching and to them.

Purpose will move you to come in early, stay late, do additional research on activities that will make your lesson plan exciting. Purpose drives us to go the extra mile even when we may not feel like it. It drives us to stay up late when we are tired and would rather be in bed; it drives us to stop by the teacher's store on a Saturday morning for supplies when we could be doing any number of other things to relax; and it drives us to make those phone calls and emails to parents with positive feedback before a call about a problem is necessary. Purpose increases creativity, self-determination, faith in our students and so much more.

Mrs. Ritchie was very clear about her purpose. She knew that children needed more than book knowledge. As a result, she was loving, compassionate, committed, charismatic, forward-thinking, funny, hardworking and a pillar of strength. Because she embodied these characteristics, she made us feel proud, hopeful, loved, safe, secure, unstoppable and perhaps most importantly, significant. The magic of her teaching was wrapped up in her deep sense of purpose for being there for us.

What's your purpose for becoming a teacher? What effect do you want to have on your students? What adjectives would they use to describe you? These are questions you must consider and reconsider, visit and revisit if the master teacher within you is to be released.

Principle 2

Conviction:
The Belief That You Can Make a Difference

Teachers are Heroes because they are filled with compassion.

All I could see was blurry numbers all over my paper as I looked through tear-stained eyes. None of these numbers made any sense, especially when it came to learning to multiply them. I just couldn't get it. It was so frustrating not being able to keep up with the other students. How come they could do it and I couldn't? What seemed to come naturally and easily to other students came painfully and with difficulty for me. So there I sat, dejected, head down on the desk, not knowing what to do. This wasn't the first time I put my head down on the desk in discouragement. As a matter of fact, it was beginning to be a pattern.

Mrs. Ritchie came over to my desk, unbeknownst to me. My head was down on the desk and I was sobbing. She didn't know about the repeated, devastating verbal abuse I was experiencing at home, even when I did do well at school. I was called "stupid" and "dummy" over and over until I began to think that those words described who I was. I remember I began to feel so poorly about myself that I would poke the eyes out of my own school pictures of myself with a pen. I didn't like those pictures of me looking at myself. But today all that would change. Mrs. Ritchie looked at the tiny teardrops on my paper. I felt a warm hand gently rub my back. I slowly lifted my head. Then she took my hand gently, lifting my head. She looked me in the eyes and said, "It's gonna be alright, Mark. You'll get it. You just have to keep trying. You are phenomenal and I believe in you. You're going to be great one day!"

Soon after this experience, I began raising my head more often, and putting forth more effort despite the difficulty. Mrs. Ritchie had tapped my spirit and touched my soul with simple

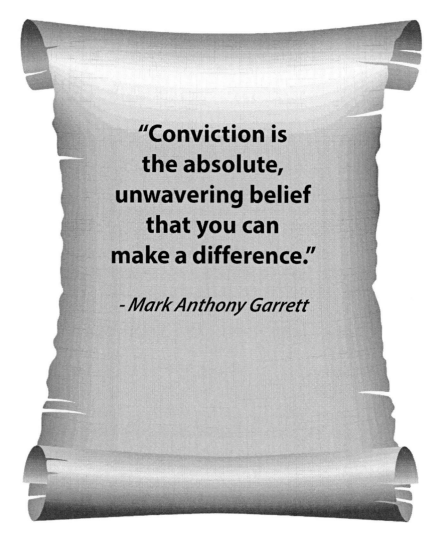

"Conviction is
the absolute,
unwavering belief
that you can
make a difference."

- Mark Anthony Garrett

words of encouragement. This is one of many things that made this incredible teacher a hero to me and countless others students

The headlines have been blazing for the past couple of years with cheating scandals in urban school districts. Superintendents, principals and teachers have been indicted leaving parents angered and students disillusioned. These cheating scandals are indicative of a larger problem—the lack of faith in the students to learn. This is why principle number two, conviction, is so important. If these educators truly believed in their own abilities and the abilities of their students, they would not have participated in cheating scandals to boost standardized test scores. Nothing increases student achievement like great teachers and great teaching!

Conviction is the absolute, unwavering belief that you can make a difference. Conviction is a two-sided coin; it is a belief in yourself as the teacher and the belief that your students can learn regardless of past performance, socioeconomic status or parental involvement. Please don't misunderstand me—these things do play a critical role in the development of a child; however, the teacher makes all the difference. This is why it's important to **teach from *potential* rather than *appearances*.** Let me explain.

Dr. Myles Munroe has defined potential as "what you can do but have not done yet." So you may have a child who has the potential to be outstanding in math, but (s)he came to you struggling in math. If you focus on the appearance of what (s)he doesn't know, (s)he will only get worse. But if you focus on the child's potential, encourage and nurture it, the child will come alive with achievement.

It is easy to become overwhelmed and exhausted by the demands of teaching. It can be tedious teaching the same materials, encountering the same types of problems with a new set of students every year. However, regardless of how many years you've been teaching, it is incumbent upon you to greet every new group of students you encounter with the same level of enthusiasm you had when you first began.

Teachers are Heroes because they believe in the children they teach.

There are many factors—societal, familial, environmental and otherwise—that play a significant role in a student's performance at school. Some of these things may be completely out of your ability to control or even impact. You can never fully know the circumstances or influences by which students are driven that creates an environment in which they make poor choices. However, simply keep in mind that these choices should not preclude them from being treated with compassion and support.

Absolute belief is contagious: the more you believe, the more the children will believe it of themselves. When children realize that you believe in their ability to succeed, the more effort they will put forth because of your belief in them. So make it your mission to demonstrate your belief in your students by creating opportunities for small victories. How about a phone call, email or note home for something good instead of bad? How about encouraging words when homework is turned in or a question is answered correctly during instruction? These things go a long way to help students understand that you expect them to succeed and that you're on their side.

A 2006 survey regarding High School Student Engagement found that one in five students disagreed with this statement. "There is at least one adult in my school who cares about me and knows me well." Considering that most high school students work with multiple teachers every day, that means that there are a lot of missed opportunities for teachers to engage and connect with

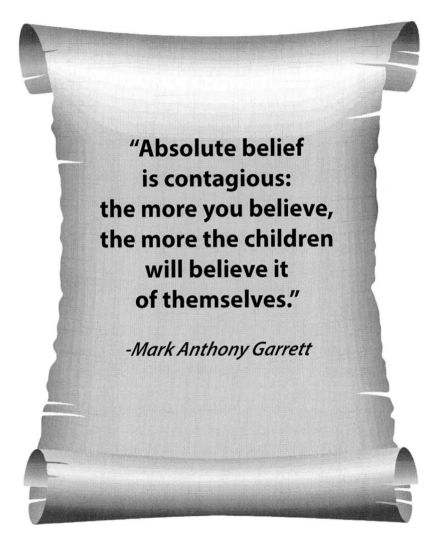

"Absolute belief
is contagious:
the more you believe,
the more the children
will believe it
of themselves."

-Mark Anthony Garrett

students. Your students, especially the most problematic ones, are starving for someone to believe in them. So many children have been told that they are worthless, that they are incapable and some have even been told that they are downright bad. There are some who feel that no one in their entire lives has ever believed in them.

Here's the question:
What reason do these students have to try when everyone expects them to fail?

Teachers are Heroes because they believe failure is not an option.

Something used to prevent a true conviction from occurring is a preconceived idea about what a student or a class can achieve. No matter what has happened previously, teachers should not permit themselves to be hoodwinked into listening to experiences that other teachers have had with other students (remember, we talked earlier about the lounge mafia). Your ability to keep an open mind about a particular student may enable you to reach a student that perhaps may not have been reached by a previous teacher.

Consider how powerful it could be to forget everything you know about a student's past performance and just believe that that student has the ability to succeed. How might they respond, when time after time and even test after test, you still choose to believe that they can succeed? Is this something that could possibly spark a change in that student's behavior?

It can take time for a student to work through years of being told "you can't" before they finally believe in the idea "you can." Sometimes, students do not perform well because they simply do not have the basic skills they need to perform.

Having absolute belief isn't only about benefiting your students. You may discover that when you truly believe in your own power to make a difference in the lives of others, you will experience less stress and more joy in your work. The absolute belief that becomes a part of your mental psyche will encourage you to press on. A state mandated curriculum at times may seem like it gets in the way of real learning. It's no wonder that students are bored when teachers are (understandably) uninspired as well. But Teachers Are Heroes because they can make that which is uninteresting on the surface fascinating because of their creative approach. This creative approach is born of a conviction that they can and are making a difference.

So try bringing more of yourself into the classroom. At the very least, you can have more fun. Students will notice the difference and you may find that there is time to cover everything when your students have more interest and are more engaged because of their connection to you. Your absolute belief in them will translate into them having absolute belief in themselves, their abilities and in your ability to teach them!

Principle 3

Passion:
Fuel Your Success With Passion and Enthusiasm

Teachers are Heroes because they are designed to inspire.

Walking into Mrs. Ritchie's class was the highlight of every day at school. Walking into her classroom was like walking into a magical wonderland, not just because of the colorful things on the wall, but because her passion and enthusiasm were unmatched. And her passion and enthusiasm permeated the energy in the classroom. She told us we were kings and queens and that the classroom was our kingdom. She put heart and soul in to everything she did and it showed in the way she interacted with us. Everyone could feel it and that's why everyone loved being in her class.

Anyone who knows me or has seen me speak to teachers, foster care providers or youth knows that I am passionate about helping young people. That passion and enthusiasm are in every fiber and cell of my body and being. Here's why: I know the power of having one adult in your life who cares, who sees past your faults and speaks to the promise of your future. I also know the devastating results of not having such an adult to give you such guidance. You see, I've lived both lives. Life is challenging enough when you have the right support systems in place, but when you don't, trying to find success is like chasing the wind—you can never quite grasp it.

Teachers are Heroes because they love what they do.

What sets teachers who are heroes apart from others is their infectious passion and enthusiasm. It was the great ancient African sage Ptahhotep who said, "Love for the work they do brings men and women closer to the Divine." The reason I have

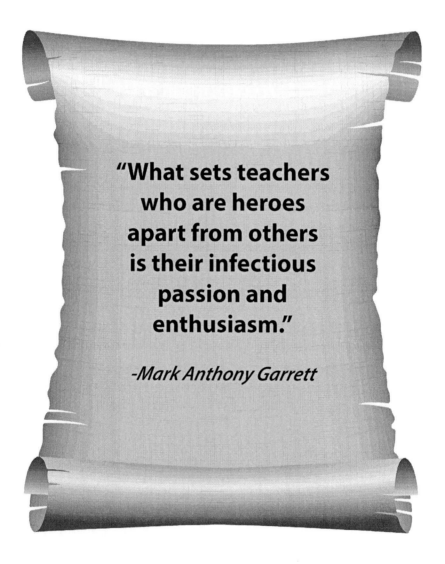

"What sets teachers who are heroes apart from others is their infectious passion and enthusiasm."

-Mark Anthony Garrett

passion and enthusiasm is also because I know how blessed I am to be alive and to be in a position to serve others. In addition, I know that one word of encouragement, one handshake, one hug can literally save a life. There are times I have shared my story in which a child confided that my story literally prevented them from committing suicide that day.

What makes you passionate and enthusiastic about teaching? Whatever it is, it should drive everything you do. Teachers who are passionate and enthusiastic have a certain spirit and energy about them that is magnetic. It draws and attracts children to them. Get in touch and in tune with your passion for teaching because here's the thing—children are master psychologists. *They know and can tell immediately whether you want to be there, whether you like what you do and whether you care for them.*

One of the best ways to sustain your passion is by surrounding yourself with individuals of like mind and like thought. If you surround yourself with passionate individuals, your energy and your enthusiasm will become contagious, plus you will push each other to levels of exemplary action.

When those around you are passionate, they will share your eagerness to engage in further discussions about teaching and the manner in which it can be done best.

They will want to analyze problems with which both you and your students are confronting on a daily basis in an effort to discuss creative and innovative ways and approaches to resolve them.

Furthermore, they will be supportive of your classroom efforts. Trying to sustain passion among jaded teachers only results in frustration and resentment on both ends. Seek out those teachers who share a similar outlook. If they are not present in your school, find them in the larger community or even on the Internet. The more you can associate with individuals, who are passionate about teaching, the more you will feed the passion within yourself.

In an article called "Nurturing Passionate Teachers," Randall Wisehart said, "Becoming a passionate teacher is more than merely being passionate about skills, content and the habits of the mind we may wish to engender in our students. First and foremost, it means making a commitment to recreating oneself as an educator—and continuing that regenerative process throughout a career." Simply put, passion is a way of life. It is not a sometime thing. It is an all the time thing.

Passion does not live on routine and familiarity. Boredom inspires no one. Trying something new once in a while can be an energizing and invigorating experience both for you and for your students. When there is a modification in the routine, students naturally perk up and respond to the change with a renewed sense of engagement and energy. Their interest is peaked because they want to know what's going to happen. This is an opportunity you can take full advantage of by making it a meaningful and memorable experience. When new ideas prove to be successful, quickly add this to your storehouse of knowledge as something that works at least for that group of students.

In a similar vein, passion must be fed by continued learning, both within the educational field as well as within your subject matter. Research is constant and ongoing (we'll talk about this more in the next chapter). To ignore changes to the field is to make you a less effective teacher. That is not to say that you must implement the ideas of every new study, but rather you stay up-to-date within the field so you can learn to discern how new research may be useful in your own classroom.

Furthermore, staying involved with your subject matter helps you to maintain your passion. You can be reminded of why you were inspired to learn about the subject in the first place. And even more so, through devoting yourself to continual learning you remind yourself what it is like to be a student.

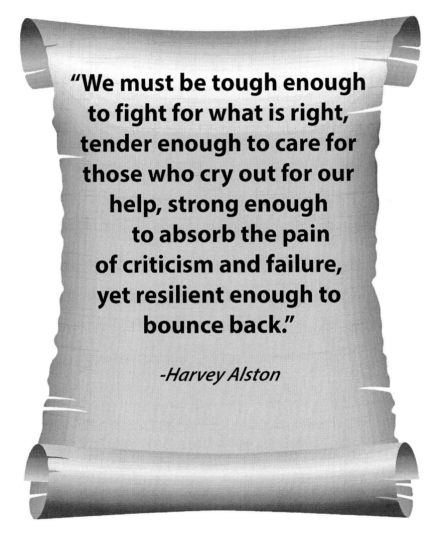

"We must be tough enough to fight for what is right, tender enough to care for those who cry out for our help, strong enough to absorb the pain of criticism and failure, yet resilient enough to bounce back."

-Harvey Alston

Lastly, passion cannot only be maintained with resilience. When it comes to passion, I am often reminded of a very powerful quote that was penned by my colleague, friend and tremendously captivating empowerment speaker, Harvey Alston, when he said, "We must be tough enough to fight for what is right, tender enough to care for those who cry out for our help, strong enough to absorb the pain of criticism and failure, yet resilient enough to bounce back." Truer words were never spoken.

As a teacher who pursues excellence, there will be many times that you expend a lot of energy and it will not always look like you are receiving a return on your investment. Your passion must be constantly fueled by your purpose and by your conviction. As a teacher, you must develop a thick skin for not always meeting with absolute success. In a single day, with the same energy and the same material, you may engage one class spectacularly while only receiving a mediocre or completely bland response from another. This is life in the classroom.

Your passion cannot rest on these experiences or individual events. You must be able to see past the world of appearances. Your passion must depend on a more general evaluation of the performance and the response of your students. At the same time, even though you know your energy may fall flat, you must still commit to passion for every class. Resilience means your knowing that the lack of clear-cut success is only temporary and that you have decided to persevere in spite of the temporary setbacks.

The following story by Chad McKibben not only demonstrates the principle of conviction that we discussed in the last chapter, it also demonstrates the passion and enthusiasm his coach had for those under his tutelage.

"Whatever You Do In This Life – Make it Count"
By Chad McKibben

Before we examine the next principle, pause for a bit and ponder, reflect and meditate on why you have chosen to be a part of this profession. Or even think for a while on why this profession has chosen you.

Chad McKibben tells a story of a teacher and a coach who had a profound impact upon his life. He takes his time and explains exactly how it happened. Here is Chad's story.

> *It was the early fall of 1991 and I found my- self driving towards the accomplishment of a life- long dream to play college baseball. I had signed with Mt. Vernon Nazarine College and in my own thoughts, I was heading to play baseball with a bunch of choir boys. I would be arriving in a new town, playing for a new team and learning from a new coach. Little did I know, the coach that awaited me would change my life forever. I'm hon- ored to introduce you to Coach Keith Veale.*
>
> *Coach Veale is the most accomplished coach in Mt. Vernon's history, but he wouldn't say that. In 21 years of coaching, he has led his teams to over 700 victories, but he would say he has great players to coach. He has won coach of the year honors on the conference, regional and national levels over 15 times, but he would say he has an incredible sup-*

porting cast. He has helped countless new recruits make the difficult journey from boyhood to becoming a man in just four short years, but he would say it is his life that has been changed.

Under the helm of Coach Veale, I quickly learned two overwhelming truths: The "Choir Boys" could really play some baseball, and there was much more to life than just the game of baseball. When Coach would talk to us before the game, he would do it with such conviction and passion. He would tell us, "You may only have one opportunity to execute, one pitch that you can drive, or one ball you need to catch; make it count." After encouraging us in our abilities and preparing us for competition, we always did the same thing next; we would all circle up, take a knee, grab a hand and say the Lord's Prayer together. After the game, win or lose, Coach would take a moment to tell us what we did well and help us to understand where we needed to grow. There is no doubt my ability and knowledge of the game increased under Coach Veale, but that's not why I want to thank him. I want to thank him for using the game of baseball to ultimately change my life.

Coach Veale was more to me and the other players than just a coach. When we were missing home and just needed to talk, he would listen. He was a listener. When we doubted our abilities on the field or in the classroom, he would encourage us. He was an encourager. When we had questions about God and our faith, biblically he would provide answers for us to think about. He was a provider. Also, when the time came for him to discipline us for various matters, he would do just that. I wouldn't really call him a disciplinarian though; he was more like a father.

It was through these opportunities I noticed Coach Veale's quiet strength. Very rarely would he ever raise his voice unless it was to encourage. He didn't have to. He spoke with you and to you with such confidence and candor. As I look back and think about Coach's humble strength, I know it was his incredible faith in God. No matter what circumstance or situation we faced, Coach would always speak in life lessons. Whether through baseball, school or just hardships, Coach was molding, shaping and forming us. Coach was growing us.

To this day, on my bookshelf, I have the bible Coach Veale gave me where he highlighted Ephesians 3: 16-19, "I pray that out of his glorious riches may he strengthen you with power through his Spirit in your inner being so that Christ may dwell in your hearts through faith. And I pray that you, being rooted and established in love, may have power, together with all the saints, to grasp how wide and long and high and deep is the love of Christ, and to know this love that surpasses knowledge—that you may be filled to the measure of all the fullness of God." The last thing that Coach ever wrote me was this: "Chad: Whatever you do in this life—make it count. I want to see you in Heaven. Be there! Coach Veale."

As I hold my Mount Vernon Nazarine College 1995 National Championship ring in my hand, I can't help but think about the games we played and the plays we made. But it is the imprint on my life that Coach Veale made that walks with me daily and influences me as a teacher today. Heading into my 12th year of teaching, I know it is by the grace of God that I've been given an opportunity to mold, shape and form the minds and spirits of the students I teach every day. As an educator, we have the responsibility to educate. But as a teacher, we get the opportunity to touch lives. I can only hope that through a career of teaching and coaching, I will be able to influence and affect one student's life like Coach Veale has impacted mine. This is why we teach and make it count.

In addition to Chad McKibben's moving testimonial, consider these powerful words from Dr. Robert Lawson as he speaks to the passion and enthusiasm of his 12th grade English teacher, Mrs. Lloyd.

A Tribute to a Life Changer
By Dr. Robert L. Lawson

Mr. Garrett has been writing about the power of passion and its impact on peoples' lives. This short snippet on the life of a true American hero is just one example of a teacher who has gone about her business of making a difference in the lives of others.

When others ask me the question, what teacher had the greatest impact upon your life, I have to reflect for a moment on the past. Though I've had a number of great teachers and some who would be considered brilliant, there's one who stands heads and shoulders above the rest. Her name was Mrs. Opal M. Lloyd.

The year was 1968. She was my 12th grade English teacher. Her powerful presence and the manner in which she approached both her students and her specialized discipline may have subconsciously moved me to become an English teacher just as she had become.

She was a tall, slender woman who moved with grace and elegance. One could easily tell that she knew both her subject matter and her students equally well. This woman possessed the gift of teaching and the gift of teaching possessed her. You could tell. Teaching was her passion. That was how she reached so many students who might otherwise have fallen by the wayside.

Perhaps the most uncanny thing about this woman lay in the fact that every student, and I do mean every student without exception, had total respect for this woman. Even those students who were marginal and inclined to mischief would do nothing in this woman's presence to cause her any unnecessary grief or agony. Her reputation preceded her. When you were in Opal M. Lloyd's class, your desire to learn was stoked and kindled like a white, hot fire.

She cared about her students. You could tell. She treated them all with equal respect and dignity. Perfection was in her DNA. Her expectations were high and each student rose to meet them. Her ability and her infectious and contagious enthusiasm for what she did exemplified her greatness.

When my friend and business associate, Mark Anthony Garrett called and asked if I would like to share a story about a life-changer for his new book, Teachers are Heroes, I was elated. It would be a cathartic experience for me. Mark was actually providing a wonderful vehicle for me to be able to share with the world how I actually felt about someone who had such a significant impact upon my life. I shared with Mark that in later years when I visited her and her husband, upon my departure from her driveway, I glanced back and could still see her standing in the doorway waving as my car slowly disappeared from view. That was just the caliber of person she was. Her character and her motives were above reproach. Opal M. Lloyd was a knowledgeable and powerful woman and she wielded both wisely.

Eleven years after I had acquired a Master's degree and two years prior to the acquisition of my Doctorate, I sent Mrs. Lloyd a letter and enclosed a tape series with it which I had assembled as a way to help others to maximize their full potential. It seems that has always been a passion of mine. Needless to say, Mrs. Lloyd was quite proud. I thought you might enjoy reading her letter firsthand. Out of respect for her, she will have the last word. I want to share her words of wisdom with you, just as she shared them with me. There is not one iota of doubt in my mind that it is exactly as Mark Garrett has said, "When you change a life as Mrs. Opal M. Lloyd has done, you are a hero."

It is a teacher's job to ignite the fire for learning in students. Just know that each time you do, you become a hero. My hat is off to each teacher who has the ability to do that. Mrs. Opal M. Lloyd has ignited my fire and she has passed the torch to me and I am still running, running, running...

Here is Mrs. Lloyd's letter in its exactness.

Dear Bob,

How thoughtful of you to remember us with the lovely letter at Christmas and the portfolio of "The Power to Excel." What a beautiful thought structure you have in the preparation and sharing of your secrets of power and success. Only one who is dedicated to his profession could have an insight such as you express and the desire to inspire others to the performance of their best potential.

Bill and I are so happy and honored that you shared with us this bit of your life's activities. Those are the things that continue to enrich the lives of teachers who were fortunate enough to have their paths cross with fine young men and women such as you.

Yes, I agree with you that those students who graduated from Southwestern High School—if they had the desire—could and will succeed. I never cease to be thankful that the greatest teacher of all saw fit to allow me the opportunity to spend 36 years in the public schools of Gallia County. No chain of precious memories is very long but I must say – very pleasant – all because of young people like you who have seen fit to accept the challenges that lie before them and have chosen to do something constructive about it.

In closing, thank you again for remembering us and we shall look forward to having you stop by sometime to call on us. May I share with you these favorite words from Ann Landers. "May fortune not forsake you; (I too, when young, peeped into paradise) May Time, The Watchman, never overtake you; Nor cau-

tion dull the mischief in your eyes. No matter what the whim of Fate denies, No matter how the years may bump and blunder, God in His mercy keep your shining eyes Glued to the knothole of eternal wonder."

Most Sincerely,
Mrs. Opal M. Lloyd

Principle 4

Consistent Improvement:
Commit To Constant & Never-Ending Improvement

Take a look at the cube below. If you look in the center of the cube, you will see a rectangle. If you stare at the rectangle, something incredible will happen. The shape will shift and you will immediately see it from a different angle. Take a moment to see the shift.

Did you see the shift? Some see it right away. For others, it may take a moment. But here's the key—to see it, you must take

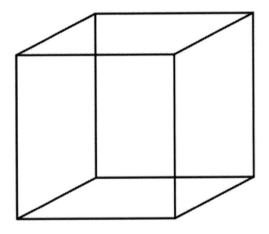

the time. The image you saw when you first looked at the cube is the common culture, the default program—the way everyone tends to see things. But once you took the time to make the shift, that represents the perspective of seeing a student (and yourself) as a magnificent success.

Their perspective allows them to see creatively with more breadth and depth. Average instructors look for what's wrong with a child. *Teachers are Heroes because they see what's right in a child and accentuate the positive.*

The average instructor sees a child with problems. *Teachers are Heroes because they see a child with possibility.* Average instructors believe many will fail naturally no matter what they do. Teachers are Heroes because they believe everyone can succeed and create a climate and culture for success in the classroom. Average instructors see students as they are. Teachers are Heroes because they see a child as (s)he can be—and lovingly call it forth.

It's imperative that you make the shift. The alternative perspective is always there waiting to be revealed. When it comes to transformational teaching, it requires a commitment to constant and never-ending improvement.

In many schools of education, in one of the first classes, students are often asked, "Is teaching an art or a science?" A deep philosophical discussion ensues as students state their position and try to justify it. However, in truth, teaching is both an art and a science. It is an art in that masterful teaching requires an endless well of creativity and to see a master teacher at work is to behold a masterpiece in the making as (s)he meticulously molds and shapes minds. It is a science in that precise methods can yield calculable and replicable results. Inquiry is the engine that drives science.

Asking the right questions can propel you on a journey to mastery. Questions like: *How do my students learn best? What are their learning styles? How can I make this topic fun? What activity can I add to this lesson? What have other teachers who served the population that I serve done to increase student achievement?*—these are the questions that lead to results. Mastery is not a mystery for those who are willing to consciously, continuously and systematically seek answers to the difficult questions.

But be mindful, no master teacher has ever been satisfied with remaining at their current level of proficiency. While others are complaining and blaming, teachers that are heroes are questioning and probing how they can do better. They are always striving to elevate their skills to another level regardless of what others are doing. People tell me all the time how much they enjoy my presentations—but I'm not satisfied. I'm always researching how I

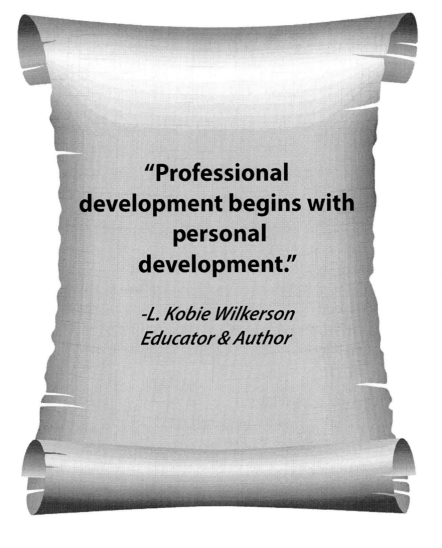

"Professional development begins with personal development."

-L. Kobie Wilkerson
Educator & Author

can do better! If we want kids to go above and beyond, shouldn't we?

This is why the ancient African sage Ptahhotep taught that "No artist ever possesses that perfection to which (s)he should aspire." And so we strive. We strive to learn, grow and experience new creative, intellectual and professional horizons. Perhaps this is why award-winning educator and author L. Kobie Wilkerson says, "Professional development begins with personal development." We should all be striving to better ourselves in every way.

Chuck Gallozzi suggests that "We all have an innate desire to endlessly learn, grow, and develop. We want to become more than what we already are. Once we yield to this inclination or continuous and never-ending improvement, we lead a life of endless accomplishments and satisfaction."

In teaching and anything important in life, in order to win, first, you must learn to LOSE. LOSE. is an acronym which simply stands for the Law of Slight Edge. This theory suggests that small, daily, incremental shifts in thought and action lead to big, monumental results. So you must commit to constant never-ending improvement. This commitment must take you significantly beyond professional development the school or school system provides.

- What are you reading?
- What teacher websites are you surfing?
- What's the latest research in your field that you've reviewed?
- What master teachers are you observing?
- What conferences are you attending or planning to attend?
- If you have a significant number of Hispanic/Latino students, have you taken the time to learn Spanish?
- What do you know about the authentic culture of the students you teach?

- What do you know about the social culture of your students (hip-hop, pop, YouTube, Facebook, Twitter)?
- How can you use Facebook, YouTube and Twitter to engage your students at deeper levels?
- Have you examined the relationship between culture and achievement and how culture can be used as a bridge rather than a barrier?
- Have you examined the nine multiple intelligences?
- Have you noted that most schools only teach to one or two of the intelligences, yet children come to school with eight or more (several of which go unstimulated in your students who are typically the most challenging)?
- Have you looked at how you can use differentiated instruction to teach to the learning styles of all the students in your class?

You already devote a lot of time and energy to the classroom. It may feel as if your responsibilities as a teacher are already encroaching on your personal time. This being so, you may have little incentive to take on extra tasks to further your professional development. Combined with unsupportive administration and problematic students, voluntarily choosing to spend more time on teaching can seem like a fool's errand.

I'm not here to tell you that you must eat, breathe and sleep teaching. Nor am I here to tell you that you must sacrifice the time off that you have earned in order to become a better teacher. What I do wish to impart is that great teachers always have improvement in the back of their minds. When they aren't actively working on themselves, they are assessing their performance and determining their strengths and weaknesses. Great teachers know that there is no such thing as a "pinnacle of success," that as long as you commit to continual improvement, there is always the possibil-

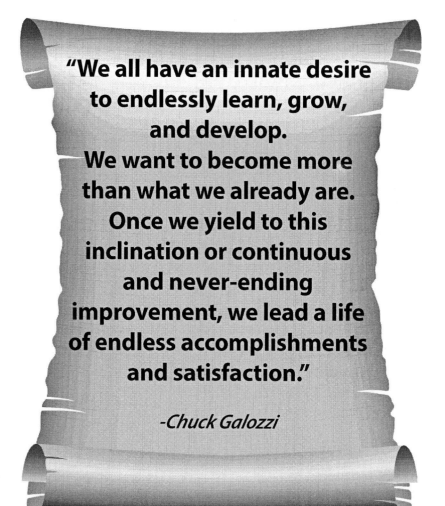

"We all have an innate desire to endlessly learn, grow, and develop.
We want to become more than what we already are.
Once we yield to this inclination or continuous and never-ending improvement, we lead a life of endless accomplishments and satisfaction."

-Chuck Galozzi

ity of reaching something greater.

When we talk about improvement, we are not talking about drastic changes. It's not about obtaining another degree (unless you want to), and it's not about performing a major overhaul to your teaching style. Nor is it about raising student test scores by a few points or taking extra responsibilities at school. While all of these things are worthy in their own right, what really matters are the small effectively invisible things you can be doing on a daily basis to become a better teacher and a better person.

Jeff Olson is the author of a book called The Slight Edge. In it, he discusses the way in which people de-motivate themselves out of their own improvement. When we think about improvement, we tend to look at the big picture and become overwhelmed at how much work it entails. Olson suggests approaching self-improvement in tiny increments. In fact, he suggests breaking them down into steps; so small, that as you complete them, it doesn't even feel like you've accomplished anything. Halfway in, sometimes you don't have time to complete a task, then you aren't left with a feeling of guilt or disappointment in yourself, because the loss of that at times seems inconsequential.

He provides the following example: a great and easy way to improve as a teacher (and in life overall) is to read. What if you read only 10 pages a day of an educational or self-improvement book? Even if you only read 250 days a year (or about two out of every three days), you could read between eight and 12 books per year. That's a lot of potentially valuable and motivational information you could be digesting.

Similarly, what if you spend 10 minutes a day doing something to improve yourself—perhaps learning another language, organizing your home or keeping up with the news—at the end of the year, you would have spent over 60 hours working on that project. If there is a day in which you can't read 10 pages, or you

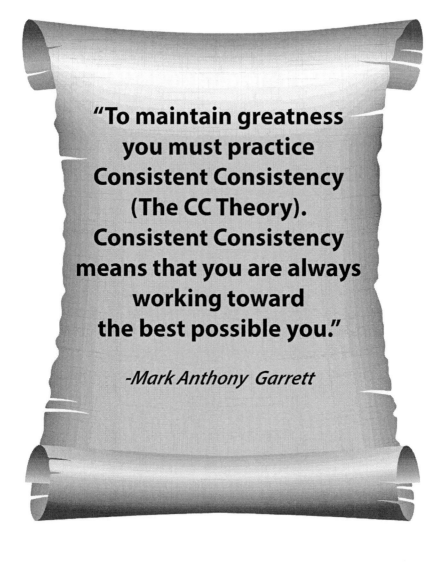

"To maintain greatness you must practice Consistent Consistency (The CC Theory). Consistent Consistency means that you are always working toward the best possible you."

-Mark Anthony Garrett

can't spend 10 minutes working on a project, that's OK. In the grand scheme of things, it doesn't matter. But when you make a habit of spending that time, over the long-term, the time adds up. What have you been meaning to do, but keep putting it off because the idea seems too overwhelming?

How can you apply the Law of Slight Edge theory (LOSE) to help you accomplish your goal? That goal? To increase and improve yourself, check out the following books:

Developing Character for Classroom Success
Aberjoulie, Charlie (2000)

Education for Transformation: The Keys to Releasing the Genius Of African American Students
Akua, Chike (2012)

The Essential 55: Rules for Discovering the Successful Student in Every Child
Clark, Ron (2004)

Dreamkeepers: Successful Teachers of African American Children
Ladson-Billings, Gloria (1994)

Teaching to Capture and Inspire All Learners
Peters, Stephen (2008)

Jaime Escalante: Inspirational Math Teacher
Schraff, Anne (2008)

This is just a list to get you started and whet your appetite. We encourage students to always have a book that they're reading…what about us? These books contain transformational, game-changing information—stories, concepts, instructional strategies and research that will help you elevate your teaching so that you can help your students be their best. While it seems like devoting time to reading will take more time out of your life, it will actually add more vitality and effectiveness to what you do. That effectiveness will increase your passion and enthusiasm that we discussed in the last chapter. It's all connected. It's all possible. As a matter of fact, all things are possible, available, and achievable to those that believe.

Your learning is never complete. There is always something more to learn about yourself, the world and how you interact. And while you can be putting forth your best effort, that does not mean that you have reached the best that you can ever be. Your best effort builds upon your past best efforts, so what your best is today may be less than your best in six months because you've grown. Success is a process. There is no to-do list for greatness, where once you've checked off all the tasks, you can consider yourself successful and coast through the rest of life. To maintain greatness, you must practice Consistent Consistency (CC theory).

Consistent Consistency means that you are always working toward the best possible you. It means you don't accept "good enough" as a life philosophy and you never believe that you are beyond improvement. The world is constantly changing; in order to maintain your place in the world, you have to change with it. Like the LOSE theory, Consistent Consistency is not about moving mountains. It's about the small moments. There are hundreds of times a day when we are presented with choices.

Among those choices, there are those that move us forward and those that keep us stagnant. Do you eat an apple or a bag of potato chips? Do you splurge on a new shirt or put money in savings? Do you spend your free periods chatting with co-workers or preparing for your lessons? Consistent consistency means that you recognize those opportunities for improvement and actively choose to pursue them—perhaps not every time—but more times than not. This is exactly why, the empowerment speaker, Anthony Robbins once said, "Anything you consistently improve, you will wind up dominating."

There are no shortcuts to greatness. There is no holy grail of teaching—one method, one text, one assignment—that can magically turn you from a good teacher into an exceptional one. Nor can you be a great teacher by riding on the coattails of someone else's ideas and hard work. No matter how great a film, worksheet or textbook, it can never teach students as well as an engaged teacher.

Teachers are Heroes because they empower children to be great.

Mrs. Ritchie was very clear about expectations of excellence and improvement. We were "Special Education" students with all of the challenges and stigmas that go along with the title. But Mrs. Ritchie was always adamant. "It doesn't matter what's on the door or what label you have. You are significant. She was always clear that the standard was excellence and she held us accountable.

Mrs. Ritchie would never allow us to use our labels as an excuse. And when we had trouble with a concept or a lesson, she would not let us get discouraged. "Mistakes are a part of the process," she would always say. Mistakes were only an indication that we were one step closer to learning the lesson. She would never teach us from our problems and appearances. She always taught us from our potential and possibilities. She didn't demand perfection, she just lovingly demanded constant and never-ending improvement.

Mrs. Ritchie's demands for constant and never-ending improvement have made all the difference in my life because this is what I leaned on to make incremental changes in my life. She helped me to see that I could better myself slowly and that over time, these little improvements would make a big difference.

Principle 5

Integrity:
Make Integrity a Guiding Principle

The way teachers speak to students makes all the difference in the world. At home, I was constantly called "dummy" and "stupid." But in Mrs. Ritchie's class, there were no dummies or "stupid" kids. We were kings and queens and her class was our kingdom. She always insisted that we were going to do something great one day. She believed in us. Her integrity as a professional would not allow her to engage us any other way. She spoke greatness into us every single day, and as a result, we gradually began to believe it and display it.

Late in the year, I received some devastating news. My Dad lost his job and, as a result, we had to move. Tearfully, I told Mrs. Ritchie that I could no longer be in her class. What she told me would change my life and later save my life. She got down on one knee and looked me in the eye. "It's gonna be alright, Mark. Just don't forget what you learned here in our kingdom. Keep your chin up. One day you're gonna be great and you're gonna do something special. You are significant."

Teachers are Heroes even when no one recognizes their service to others.

We spoke in an earlier chapter about the recent problems of school system cheating scandals. We noted that this is deeply problematic because if the teachers and administrators truly believed in the children's abilities and in their own abilities to teach the children, then cheating would be unthinkable. Such behavior is also unthinkable when one has unwavering integrity. Alan Simpson tells us, "If you have integrity, nothing else matters. If you don't have integrity, nothing else matters." You see, if you have integrity, the hard work, going the extra mile, learning what works best for your students and applying it will all flow from that integ-

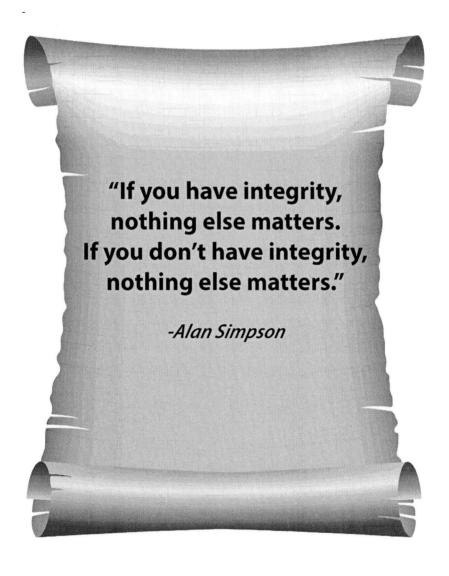

"If you have integrity,
nothing else matters.
If you don't have integrity,
nothing else matters."

-*Alan Simpson*

rity. So now, let's examine this principle on a much deeper level with some real-world examples.

Teachers are Heroes because they believe in the impossible.

There are some instructors who feel that some students are just going to fail and they think that's just the way it is. Master teachers challenge this notion by helping all of their students to succeed. Crystal Bradley reports that the beginning of her first year as a teacher was a virtual nightmare. She entered the teaching profession with overwhelming optimism and energy only to be faced with a first grade class of students who had the worst behavior and academic scores in the school.

She painstakingly put together a plan of action to increase her students' achievement, but she met with tremendous administrative resistance. She set the textbooks to the side and began differentiating instruction, using culturally relevant instructional strategies and tapping into the multiple intelligences with movement and kinesthetic activities. She called and met with parents regularly to teach them what she was teaching their children and to show them how she was teaching them, so that they could assist their children at home. When the principal came to do an observation and evaluation, Crystal was reprimanded for deviating from the textbooks. As a matter of fact, she was constantly criticized for her pedagogical practices.

Teachers are Heroes even when they are made to feel that they don't matter.

Crystal was trained by the legendary Dr. Asa Hilliard. She remembers many days coming to his office on campus literally in tears because what she was doing didn't seem to be working. She was doing everything he taught her to do—create community in the classroom, use the culture of the children as an instructional strategy, differentiate instruction, tap into the multiple intelligences and teach the parents—yet still she was misunderstood and assumed to be ineffective by her principal and colleagues.

Her methods were considered unprofessional and unorthodox—that is, until the results of the state test came back. Her class, which was easily regarded as the worst in the school at the beginning of the school year, outperformed all the other classes. Now the principal wanted to know how she was able to get these results and wanted to get her to show the other teachers in the school. She went from being on a Personal Improvement Plan to becoming a Teacher Leader and Academic Coach. All of this happened because she refused to surrender her integrity. As a result, she is leaving a legacy of excellence.

Integrity told her that all of her children could do well if she was not chained and shackled to a textbook. Integrity told her that the parents really did care, but many of them didn't know what to do to help their children. So, integrity told Crystal to hold weekly parent meetings to educate the parents on the methods to help their children succeed.

Integrity told her to first convince the students they were winners and get them in the right mindset before teaching a lesson; that way, they would be more receptive to the lesson when it was taught. Crystal has used this same method with hundreds of urban elementary, middle and high school students over the years, always producing the same results.

She has helped innumerable students jump several letter grades in a matter of weeks and months, turning mediocre achievement into mastery. All of this because of integrity. She truly knows and believes that every child can succeed…and she proves it over and over again. It's all about integrity.

Teachers are Heroes because they empower through their words and actions.

It's this same integrity that was a driving force behind the legendary feats of Jaime Escalante. Perhaps you've seen the movie "Stand and Deliver." If you haven't seen it, do yourself and favor and check it out. Jaime was a teacher in a very low-performing high school. He was told he would be teaching computer science, only to show up on the first day and discover the school had no computers and he was assigned to teach math. Serious discipline problems in the school, gang activity, drug use and truancy were daily challenges he faced while trying to teach math to Latino students.

He, too, used culturally relevant instructional strategies and related math to the real world of his students. He believed that his students, who in the past had failed basic math consistently, could learn calculus. He developed a relationship with his students and a rigorous curriculum, spending extra hours of instruction and tutoring before and after school. His students' scores were so high on the state test that they were accused of cheating. His integrity was in question and the integrity of his students.

Teachers are Heroes because they plant seeds of hope.

The reality was that no one expected students at that school to be able to perform in math at that level. Jaime Escalante turned it into a lesson for the students. He told them that no one believed they could score that high...but he believed they could, again. The students took the test again with very similar results proving the naysayers wrong. Many of his students, who never would have continued their education after high school, went on to college and successful careers while he built the Advanced Placement Math program for a number of years at the school.

Jaime Escalante's integrity would not let him give up on his students even when they gave up on themselves. Jaime Escalante's integrity would not let him give up on his students when state education authorities questioned the integrity of their scores on the state math test. His integrity made him come early and stay late, even holding classes on the weekends and during breaks because he knew what his students were capable of. As a result, he left a legacy of excellence. It's all about integrity.

The teaching profession has been under intense scrutiny over the past decade at the national level. In fact and indeed, there are many instructors who do not represent the profession well. But I still know deep down that Teachers are Heroes. While proper legislation and funding is needed and necessary to help improve our schools, I don't believe that politics or legislation can necessarily change the way we educators are viewed. It must come from the bottom up. The way we represent our profession must be done with the utmost respect and integrity because people will respond to us based on the way we carry ourselves and provide the incredible service we are called to deliver.

I know Teachers are Heroes. We just do not hear enough of their stories. I know Teachers are Heroes because I was taught by one. Plain and simple, that's why I'm still alive today to tell the story.

Teachers Are Heroes

Principle 6

Courage:
Embrace Adversities, Enjoy the Victory

Teachers are Heroes because they work hard, but not for the money.

Teaching is not easy, it is not predictable and it is not stress-free. There will be times in your career when you may feel worn out, discouraged and downright scared. It may be that fear and anxiety are a frequent part of your teaching day. That's all right. You have been given a lot of responsibility and when you truly care about something, it's a natural reaction to be nervous. Teaching is a test of bravery—not just on your first day, but in every class. Courage is essential, to carry you through each day, but even more so, to help you during those times when you feel most defeated.

People tend to see challenges as roadblocks—things in the way of a particular goal that must be eliminated or circumvented in order to proceed. While challenges can certainly halt progress, they are also the point at which innovation is made. Every time you face a new problem, it is an opportunity. If the problem is of a more personal nature, it provides the space for you to learn about yourself and grow in the process. If it is one of a more professional nature, then it gives you a chance to bring forth your creativity.

Every time you encounter a problem, it is a sign that something in the current system is not working. Welcome these challenges, allow them to inspire self-reflection. Chike Akua has noted that "master teachers are able to transcend politics, policies, paperwork and procedures to meet the needs of the students." This means that we cannot let the kinks in the bureaucracy keep us from being our best.

By reassessing things every time you encounter a new problem, you safeguard against becoming too settled and prevent yourself from disengaging from your students, your classroom and your

"Accept the challenges
so that you may feel
the exhilaration
of victory."

-General George S. Patton

own performance. Furthermore, these moments are important to help you work through such issues. It allows you to create distance from the problem so you can focus less on your frustration and more on developing a solution.

One of the most courageous things a teacher can do after examining the performance of his or her students is to be honest with themselves. Sometimes, the most challenges thing to do is to acknowledge, "What I'm doing is not working." But you can't leave it at that. The real courage comes in when you take the time to learn how to fix whatever is broken. Is it discipline and classroom management? Is it instructional strategies? Is it connecting with students? Is it understanding the role culture plays in student achievement? Is it managing the workload? Or is it a combination of all of these?

One thing that can help with just about all of these is understanding students' learning styles and multiple intelligences. Howard Gardner developed his theory of multiple intelligences, suggesting that children have a wide range of cognitive abilities. He noted nine areas of abilities that deserve particular attention and that children tend to be outstanding in more than one.

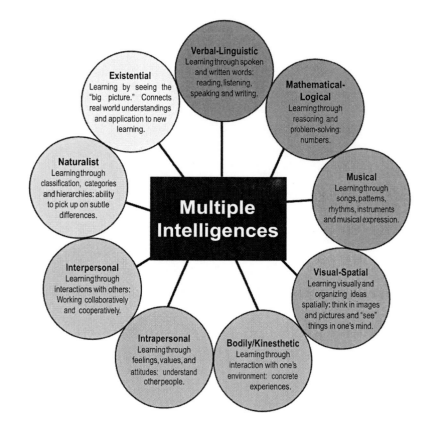

www.pbs.org lists and defines the
Nine Multiple Intelligences as follows:

Howard Gardner's Nine Multiple Intelligences

1. **Linguistic Intelligence (Word Smart):** the capacity to use language to express what's on your mind and to understand other people. Any kind of writer, orator, speaker, lawyer or other person for whom language is an important stock in trade has great linguistic intelligence.

2. **Logical/Mathematical Intelligence (Logic Smart):** the capacity to understand the underlying principles of some kind of causal system, the way a scientist or a logician does; or to manipulate numbers, quantities, and operations, the way a mathematician does.

3. **Musical Rhythmic Intelligence (Music Smart):** the capacity to think in music; to be able to hear patterns, recognize them, and perhaps manipulate them. People who have strong musical intelligence don't just remember music easily, they can't get it out of their minds, it's so omnipresent.

4. **Bodily/Kinesthetic Intelligence (Body Smart):** the capacity to use your whole body or parts of your body (your hands, your fingers, your arms) to solve a problem, make something, or put on some kind of production. The most evident examples are people in athletics or the performing arts, particularly dancing or acting.

5. **Spatial Intelligence (Picture Smart):** the ability to represent the spatial world internally in your mind—the way a sailor or airplane pilot navigates the large spatial world, or the way a chess player or sculptor represents a more circumscribed spatial world. Spatial intelligence can be used in the arts or in the sciences.

6. **Naturalist Intelligence (Nature Smart):** the ability to discriminate among living things (plants, animals) and sensitivity to other features of the natural world (clouds, rock configurations). This ability was clearly of value in our evolutionary past as hunters, gatherers, and farmers; it continues to be central in such roles as botanist or chef.

7. **Intrapersonal Intelligence (Self Smart):** having an understanding of yourself; knowing who you are, what you can do, what you want to do, how you react to things, which things to avoid, and which things to gravitate toward. We are drawn to people who have a good understanding of themselves. They tend to know what they can and can't do, and to know where to go if they need help.

8. **Interpersonal Intelligence (People Smart):** the ability to understand other people. It's an ability we all need, but is especially important for teachers, clinicians, salespersons, or politicians—anybody who deals with other people.

9. **Existential Intelligence (Spirit Smart):** the ability and proclivity to pose (and ponder) questions about life, death and ultimate realities.

Here's the key: Gardner believed that most teachers and most schools only teach to one or two of the intelligences (Linguistic and Logical-Mathematical), leaving much of a child's abilities and potential untapped. Children whose abilities do not fall in the Linguistic or Logical-Mathematical categories may begin to withdraw, lack interest or become discipline problems.

So it's one thing to know the multiple intelligences. However, it takes courage and commitment to recognize and improve upon your ability to teach to each of the nine multiple intelligences. In the classroom of a teacher who is a hero, you will find the delivery of lessons and activities that can elevate and illuminate each of these intelligences, thereby giving children the ability to shine in their own unique ways.

Another area that requires courage is an understanding of the role culture plays in student achievement. Educational research has demonstrated that culture is the key—the critical mediating factor in increasing student achievement, especially among children of color. Yet in the area of low student achievement, many blame the children rather than understanding the mistakes of the schools who serve them. This is not an attempt to excuse absent or ineffective parenting which exists in some cases. That would be subject matter for an entirely different book. This is an attempt to examine what can be done by teachers who care—teachers who are heroes. This puts you back into a position of empowerment as one who can make a difference.

So Gloria Ladson-Billings developed her model of culturally relevant teaching in her book Dreamkeepers and noted that when teachers are not culturally competent, they will often not know how to capitalize on the cultural strengths of their students— cultural strengths like: pride, resilience, hard work, cooperation, creativity, values, etc.

As one who is called to speak at very diverse functions for schoolchildren and foster-care children, the nature of what I do requires me to assess audiences of hundreds of children on the spot and speak to their spirit. While there are certainly universal principles which tap the spirit and touch the souls of all people, there are specific methods and modalities that peak the potential and performance of particular cultural groups. In an increasingly diverse world, cultural competence is not optional but essential. So here are a few simple and basic things you can do to make yourself more culturally competent:

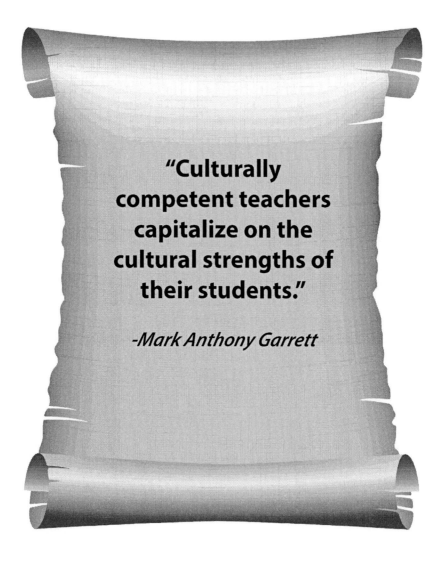

"Culturally competent teachers capitalize on the cultural strengths of their students."

-Mark Anthony Garrett

1. **Educate yourself in the cultures of the children you serve (and all cultures).** Education leads to understanding and appreciation. Once you begin to better understand and appreciate all cultures, you will have a thirst to learn more and want to share it with others.

2. **Use culture as a *bridge* rather than a barrier.** For centuries, due to ignorance, cultural differences have divided people because of misinformation and misunderstandings. You can use culture as a bridge by exposing children to the beauty of different cultures.

3. **Consistently elevate and celebrate *the best* of the culture of the children you teach throughout the year.** Pop media tends to expose the worst of certain cultures—crime, poverty, thuggishness, etc. Your students will see this because they consume pop media through television, movies and social media. So you must show them the best of the different cultures you teach about and be able to demonstrate each cultures contributions to math, science, technology, literature or whatever discipline you teach.

It takes courage to acknowledge that there are some things we need to improve on. It takes even more courage to correct some of our mistakes so that our children can receive the best education possible. It's been my experience that when you take the time to get to know and teach to your students' culture, learning styles and intelligences, they will appreciate you more and go out of their way to increase their effort and achievement. You've heard it said before, "Children don't care how much you know until they know how much you care."

Principle 7

Persistence:
Unleash The Hero Within

Teachers are Heroes because they never give up.

Too often in this world, we associate heroism with the feats of the superhuman. We only think to admire those who react fast in a crisis or put themselves in imminent physical danger for another person. But there is another type of heroism that is even more significant.

The heroism in teaching is an unassuming kind, so unassuming that teachers themselves may not even realize when they have affected a profound change. Nevertheless, the impact is felt. There is heroism in the endurance it takes to arrive at school, day after day, commit to teaching even when faced with a lack of adequate support. There is heroism in being able to juggle hundreds of different personalities each day, creating order and growth out of looming chaos. There is heroism in putting in long hours for low pay and little thanks. There is heroism in fighting for children that at times don't even want to fight for themselves or whose parents seem to have surrendered them over to you. There is heroism in what you do every single day.

It is this type of heroism that truly matters because it's not about one moment, one life saved. It's about the hundreds of small lives that touch hundreds of students that culminate in true change. Arne Duncan, the United States Secretary of Education said recently, "I really believe that teachers are the heroes of our society—too often the unsung heroes."

When you teach, you are saving the future of society. You are actively and consistently making the world a better place. Teach every day as if you are capable of creating change because you are. You can never know how one word of encouragement might change a child's life—perhaps that day or perhaps years later. Your impact can be enormous. Believe in your own worth.

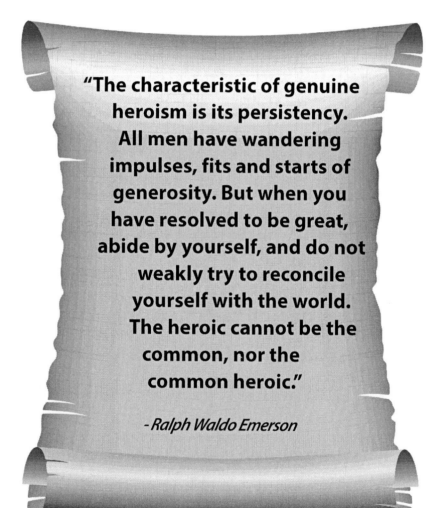

"The characteristic of genuine heroism is its persistency. All men have wandering impulses, fits and starts of generosity. But when you have resolved to be great, abide by yourself, and do not weakly try to reconcile yourself with the world. The heroic cannot be the common, nor the common heroic."

- Ralph Waldo Emerson

Believe in your own goodness and in the benefit all students will receive through your interaction with them. You are significant. Believe in the champion within. You already have the Courage and the Heart to be remarkable.

Chike Akua discovered that Teachers Are Heroes from a student who gave him a staggering compliment in the form of a question:

Sarah's Angel

It was one of my favorite stories to teach because, by extension, I could plant the seeds for some deep life lessons. I always enjoyed it because the characters were vivid and the theme was clear. Reading this story always evoked interesting class discussion and dialogue.

I had carefully prepared the class a couple of days before with the vocabulary words they would encounter in the story. We learned some background information about Asian culture. Then, on one very special day which I will never forget, we read "Waters of Gold," a Chinese folktale by Laurance Yep.

It was about a kind old woman name Auntie Lily who was poor. But she always helped people, even to her own detriment at times. She had a rich neighbor who was stingy and grumpy. One day, an old beggar came into the village pleading for water for his feet. He was dirty and grimy, covered from head to toe with filth. When he came to the rich woman's door, she said, "You'd need a whole river to wash you clean. Get out of here!" And she slammed the door. Auntie Lily, on the other hand, discreetly held her breath and asked the man how she could help him. She got him some water and offered him the little bit of food she had.

The beggar was so grateful, he told her to take the bucket of water he had washed in, cover it with a plate and look in it the next morning. To her amazement, the next morning, the bucket was

filled with gold coins.

I always enjoyed teaching this story because there were some critical character developing concepts in it. After discussing the low-level questions of who, what, when and where in the story, we then went deeper.

"Who was that man who appeared to be a beggar? Who do you think he was," I queried. The bright eyes of my seventh graders looked back with excitement. Several hands shot up.

"I think he was Jesus, because he could appear in different places like that and perform miracles," said Robert.

"I think it was the Spirit of God, because God can do stuff like that, too," said Destiny.

With each answer I nodded my head and praised them because they were thinking deeply. They had thought of spiritual answers with no prompting from me. But the story left no clear indication of who the beggar really was.

"Maybe he was really an angel because they appear to people and do miracles, don't they?" said Brittany.

"It's interesting that you say that," I replied, "because there is an ancient proverb which says, 'be careful in entertaining strangers, for many have entertained angels unaware.'"

We talked about how important it is to treat people with respect and kindness regardless of how they look or dress. We talked about how blessed and fortunate we all were since we had food to eat and nice clothes. I was very pleased with our discussion. The children's attention and participation met my expectations. I began to complete the lesson and get the class ready to go to lunch.

Then Sarah raised her hand and, probably inadvertently, gave me one of the greatest compliments I have ever received as a teacher. The compliment came in the form of a question. It seemed like such an elementary question, not one you would hear from a *middle school child. I just knew after she asked it that the whole class would burst into laughter and tease her for asking such a question. But they didn't. They got completely silent and stared at me waiting intently for an answer. It was the loudest silence I have ever heard in all my life.*

With eyes open wide and a look of awe-inspiring expectancy on her face, she said, "Mr. Akua, are you an angel?"

I was floored by the question. When I declared my major in education as a freshman in college and began studying to become a teacher, I did not realize that I was signing up to have the opportunity to be an angel in the life a child. Once I regained my composure, my response was simply, "No, I'm just trying to do the work of the One who sends the angels."

Teachers are Heroes because God made them that way.

How does one end a book such as this? I can think of only one way. By allowing the words of two of your most powerful allies and most powerful advocates to share their stories on how teachers influenced their lives.

Perhaps, when you read Wheatley S. Davis's and Elyse Chantal's stories, you will realize the significance of your role as a teacher and your potential to be the difference maker in the lives of millions of children around this nation.

It is my fervent hope and prayer that Wheatley's and Elyse's words will touch your heart, as they have mine, and that you will take some time to reflect on what they have to say. Perhaps you had one of these girls in your classroom. How did you handle it? The youth of America and the youth around the world need your expertise and they need it on a daily basis. Here are their stories.

To Sra. T, With Love

Wheatley S. Davis

"What is my student number?"

It was the first day of high school and I was being asked for my identification number more often than my name. The middle to high school transition is challenging enough, but I was making the jump to a high school of over 5,000 students. While this alone was intimidating, it paled in comparison to the leap I had just made from living in a small northern lakeside town to a sprawling western Detroit suburb.

I remember feeling saddened that my identification was now simply a number—my name didn't seem to carry as much relevance in this mammoth-sized school with overcrowded halls.

But then, I went to Spanish class.

Her name was Sra. (translates to Mrs. in English) Throneberry. She was waiting at her door to greet us with a welcoming smile and her room felt homey, comforting. She started class by commanding us in Spanish to do something as a group. We all giggled nervously together as we realized we had no clue what to do. She added gestures and we realized she wanted us to stand up; so we did. After some standing and sitting and more laughter, she began our first class. By the time I left her room that day, I not only felt like I belonged, but had fallen in love with a new subject. And that was only day one!

Sra. Throneberry's class was a place where we all felt cherished. She knew our names and gave us nicknames. She knew our interests as well as our passions and incorporated those into our daily lessons; *__she knew us__*. In a school and city where becoming a number or a face in a crowd was a fairly easy thing to do, she would never let that happen.

I was blessed to have Sra. T for all four years of my high school career. During that time, many

traumas and changes happened for me. I started dealing with a social anxiety disorder, my Mom had brain surgery, I was coping with the cultural shock of our move, etc. However, I always knew that when I got to Spanish class, I could breathe more easily. It felt like coming home. Sra. T didn't make us check our emotions, lives and identities
at the door, she embraced us with an unconditional love that let us knew we were in a safe, nurturing place—no matter what. I remember seeing classmates come in with tears in their eyes from a recent break-up or exhausted from overextending themselves. Rather than force them to "learn," Sra. T would put a reassuring hand on their shoulder and offer them a quiet spot at the back table or allow them to nod off in class. While she might not have taught them the day's Spanish lesson, they learned something more important by her example: ***how to be a good person***.

I had planned to be a doctor. In fact, I was pre-med up until my junior year of college, but was always a Spanish major. It was only when my
mom asked, "Do you really just want to see people when they're sick?" that I realized medicine was not where I wanted to be. As I thought back to the people who most profoundly affected me, Sra. T came instantly to my mind and heart. In my time in her classroom, I saw her positively impact more

people with her grace and love than some people touch in a lifetime. *I want to be Sra. T,* I thought.

So here I am. I just completed my sixth year of teaching Spanish and couldn't be happier with my choice. In an interesting twist, Sra. T retired the year that I started teaching. She allowed me to come back and choose from her wonderfully
whimsical assortment of classroom items, so every day when I enter my room I am reminded of one of my greatest role models. I am honored and humbled to be living her legacy and strive to be the kind of teacher she was. I still use songs she taught us. I still give stickers like she did. I even use some of her mannerisms! It is as though she is permanently embedded in my soul.

Every year I begin class the same way that Sra. T did on my first day back in ninth grade. Carrying her in my heart and passing along the passion for Spanish that she ignited in me is one of the greatest (and most humbling) honors I have ever had. Sra. T is forever part of who I am and I can never thank her enough for that.

¡Te amo, Sra. T! Thank you for sharing your heart of gold with every student that entered your classroom. You always will be one of my greatest heroes.

A Gift of Themselves
By *Elyse Chantal*

From the age of 14 to 16, I woke up every day hoping to die. Afraid to see the act through myself, I dreamed of some accident that would permanently end my misery. Perhaps some of my desperation was born out of teenage angst, but most of it arose out of true despair; despair that I would ever live without cycling through different moods countless times each day; despair that they would ever find a medication that stabilized me without destroying my body first; despair that night after night, I returned to a house that felt more like hostile territory than a home.

In those years, I clung to anything and anyone who could get me through the day. I count myself blessed that I had two amazing teachers who gave me their time, support and attention. Mr. Odell, the band teacher, and Mr. Micera, the choir teacher were the dynamic duo. They shared an office and an easy rapport . Their laughter was infectious and students flocked to their office during free periods to take part in the fun. I, in particular, was a hardcore office groupie.

It began with the music. I played flute in my high school's wind ensemble and started singing in the chorus after I became involved in the school drama productions. Music gave me a peace I couldn't find on my own. Out of a body that I despised, I could produce something beautiful. For the hard work and practice I put in, I received tangible results. And when life became overwhelming, playing my flute would take me to a calmer, more peaceful space. On the other hand, singing allowed me to transfer my pain onto the music and the lyrics. Mr. Odell and Mr. Micera are both talented musicians and passionate teachers. They fostered and encouraged my growing interest in music. But it is not the gift of music that I love them for the most.

Mr. Odell saw me every day and he was always very aware of how I was faring. He said he could see it in my eyes. At a time when I felt like my pain was invisible—or at least no one cared to notice— he was a constant, gentle reminder that someone was looking out for me. He allowed the music office to become my safe haven. I would visit during lunch, during study hall and after school. There would be times when half my day would be spent in the music wing. And if I occasionally skipped class for "flute lessons" that weren't scheduled, he let me get away with it.

He was the one adult figure in my life that I trusted to be on my side. I was suspicious of the traditional support networks in the high school and perhaps rightly so. I was missing school for psychiatric hospitalizations for medical complications arising from overmedication, and from being too exhausted and too overwhelmed to deal with life. The administrators were highly involved in my situation, and while I know they genuinely cared for me, at times they were motivated more by the school's best interest than my own.

With Mr. Odell, I never doubted that he was fully in my corner. He never pressured me. I could share my problems, or just stay silent. I could spend my free time practicing my flute, or just sit in the office while he worked. And on the few occasions he did push, I listened. At times when getting up and leaving the office felt like more than I was capable of accomplishing, his insistence that I had to go to class gave me the motivation I needed. And somehow I kept going, every day, and I knew I could always count on him to be there when I needed him.

Mr. Micera played an equally important role in my life. He has an easy way about him that makes you feel like you're best friends and it allowed him to easily gain my trust. When I opened up to him, he responded to my thoughts and feelings, not as if I was a student looking for advice, but as a person talking with a peer. He was the first person in my life who made me feel like I mattered, not for exter-

nal accomplishments, but for my internal reality. He showed me that my feelings and my experiences were valid and worthy of being respected.

In addition to being the choral teacher, Mr. Micera was also the director of the school plays, so I spent a lot of time in rehearsal. Rehearsals were a three-part blessing. First, I was acting, which was where my true passion lay. Music soothed my soul, but acting set it on fire. Acting gave me a goal beyond high school on which to focus and my times on stage were some of my only moments of unadulterated joy. The second blessing was that rehearsals got me out of my house for a few hours each night and into a space that I loved. At home, I spent most of my time locked in my room indulging and nourishing the ugly emotions that fed my illness. Rehearsals helped me to stay out of my head and encouraged me to build healthy relationships with my fellow cast members. The third blessing was that I got to spend time with someone I trusted; someone in whom I sought comfort and someone with whom I had become a bit enamored in that teenage girl sort of way.

There were times when I considered killing myself. In fact, it was a continual debate. But, it was always a commitment and a sense of loyalty to those two teachers that was the primary reason I decided against it.

"I'll do it after the concert at Carnegie Hall...after the fall play... after the winter band concert... after the spring musical... etc." I was concerned not for how my death would affect my family but how it would affect Mr. Odell and Mr. Micera. I don't think they can possibly know how deeply I love them and how important that love was in keeping me alive.

It's been six years since I've graduated high school and the power of their impact has not diminished in my memory. I visit when I can. To this day, the performing arts center feels like coming home. It's ironic. You couldn't pay me to return to high school, but, when I see them, I yearn to go back just so I could spend more time with them.

Mr. Odell and Mr. Micera go above and beyond for their students, but it was the small gestures that made all the difference. It was the gift of their attention, their time, their presence. It was the gift of themselves that saved my life.

Teachers Are Heroes

Mark with Chicago City Schools Leadership Club Members.

Mark doing his famous motorcycle dance.

Mark just chillin' with kids.

Mark hanging out with world-class educator Ron Clark.

We first saw Mr. Garrett present at a Race To The Top conference and knew we had to have him. His Teachers Are Heroes message was just what our educators needed. He was able to capture our hearts with his story and empower us to think outside the box and to think like champions. Some of us were brought to tears as his message reminded us of our significance and the very important role we play in the lives of the students we serve. Thank you Mark for sharing your heart with us.

Meghan Large, Service Learning Coordinator,
Green Local Schools

We were very fortunate to have Mark Anthony come to our district to motivate and fire up 700 of our teachers and administrators. He did an outstanding job and helped us to remember the importance of why we do what we do. Mark was a phenomenal in-service speaker and a true professional. I would HIGHLY recommend him!

Steve Gill, Principal Bethel Tate Middle School

Mark Anthony Garrett was such a fantastic speaker and inspiration for our freshmen orientation. He was able to connect with our students and staff and give them relevant strategies to help them succeed both academically and professionally. He was fun, engaging and the perfect fit for what we were looking for. We plan to have him back in the very near future.

Dr. Gregory Sojka, President Rio Grande University

Thank you Mark for inspiring our youth to be the best that they can be. Your "Heroes of Tomorrow" message reinforced to our youth that they are important and can become ANYTHING they set their minds to. Our students are still talking about your message and how fun it was. Thank you for touching the hearts of our kids.

Tamara Waterman, Project Gear-Up Coordinator

I've seen a lot of speakers during my years in education, and Mark is the best I've ever seen. The way he was able to connect with our student body and keep them on the edge of their seats was classic. As Mark shared his story about being a special needs kid and growing up in the inner city, I knew that he was inspiring the hearts of our students. They LOVED him. Thanks for being an inspiration and helping our kids to see a brighter future for themselves.

Debbie Skies, Principal Brentwood Middle School

Mark Anthony Garrett was the keynote speaker at our DHR Supervisors' Conference. His message on leadership, service excellence and being a hero for the children and families we serve was highly informational, inspiring and purposeful. He made us laugh, cry and reflect on the true meaning and importance of what we do. He helped us expand our paradigm and understand that excellence is the standard for all we do. Mark was a true professional and one of the best keynote speakers we have ever had.

Judy Hand, Program Manager University of Alabama

Teachers Are Heroes

In Closing

I hope that this book has inspired you to continue to teach with greatness. Never forget how important you are in the lives of the students you serve. Remember always that you are here on this planet for an ultimate purpose. No matter how challenging things become, NEVER GIVE UP! Keep on pushing, keep on fighting and most of all, KEEP ON BELIEVING! Thank you for being a HERO!   I will leave you with the famous words of Victor Hugo.

"In each age, men of genius undertake the ascent. From below, the world follows them with their eyes. These men go up the mountain, enter the clouds, disappear, reappear; people watch them, mark them. They walk by the side of precipices. They daringly pursue their road. See them aloft, see them in the distance; they are but black specks. On they go. The road is uneven, its difficulties constant. At each step a wall, at each step a trap. As they rise, the cold increases. They must make their ladder, cut the ice and walk on it, hewing the steps in haste. A storm is raging. Nevertheless, they go forward in their madness. The air becomes difficult to breathe. The abyss yawns below them. Some fall. Others stop and retrace their steps; there is a sad weariness. The bold ones continue. They are eyed by the eagles; the lightning plays about them, the hurricane is furious. No matter, they persevere."

About the Author

Mark Anthony Garrett grew up in the tough inner city of Dayton, Ohio as a foster child and was then later adopted. Throughout his childhood, he faced many hardships such as poverty, neglect, homelessness, abandonment and abuse, both physical and sexual. At 14, he lost his adopted mother to cancer, dropped out of school, joined a gang and was in and out of juvenile jail.

Although his surroundings were negative, Mark was encouraged by a teacher to never give up on life and to always strive for excellence. He knew he had to take destiny into his own hands. After receiving guidance from influential mentors, Mark enrolled in college and majored in wildlife biology and went on to become a two-time U.S. Achievement Academy Award Winner recipient of the National Collegiate Minority Leadership award and received the highest honors given by his college, which were the President's and Trustee's awards.

This experience inspired him to dedicate his life to helping troubled youth and adults overcome the negative challenges within their own lives and discover that they have greatness within them. Mark is extremely passionate about helping raise the mental consciousness of people all across the nation and abroad.

For over 17 years, Mark Anthony Garrett has motivated audiences from all over the world through his electrifying speeches, training and transformational seminars. Mark is a leading expert within the Child Welfare and K-12 educational industry on such topics as Staff and Foster Parent Retention, Empowerment, Leadership, Service Excellence, Overcoming Adversities, Youth Empowerment and Maximizing Human Potential.

He is best known for his premium professionalism, high-energy programs, humor, enthusiasm and the ability to captivate audi ences of all types. Mark is the owner of three successful businesses, a former international radio talk show host, actor and author of three inspirational books. He has contributed and published articles for various newspapers and publications around the country and has delivered well over 2,500 paid speeches and seminars. He is also a leading columnist for Fostering Families Today magazine. Mark is one of the most requested speakers within the Child Welfare and K-12 educational industry.